# cooking the
# VIETNAMESE way

Crunchy lettuce, cucumbers, and carrots combine with rice noodles and sliced pork in rice noodle salad. Lemon grass (shown here) gives the meat its unique, delicious flavor. (Recipe on page 22.)

# cooking the
# VIETNAMESE way

CHI NGUYEN & JUDY MONROE

PHOTOGRAPHS BY ROBERT L. & DIANE WOLFE

easy menu
*ethnic*
cookbooks

Lerner Publications Company ▪ Minneapolis

**Editor: Laura Storms**
**Drawings and Map by Jeanette Swofford**

The page border for this book is the chrysanthemum, a much-treasured flower in Vietnam. The Vietnamese consider it an honor to receive this flower, which symbolizes strength and longevity.

*To my mother and mother-in-law, who each taught me so much about cooking* – C.N.

*To Howard, whose support and trust I appreciate* – J.M.

Library of Congress Cataloging in Publication Data

Nguyen, Chi.
  Cooking the Vietnamese way.

  (Easy menu ethnic cookbooks)
  Includes index.
  Summary: An introduction to the cooking of Vietnam
featuring such recipes as spring rolls, sweet and sour
soup, and Vietnamese fried rice. Also includes information
about the land, history, and holidays of this southeast
Asian country.
  1. Cookery, Vietnamese—Juvenile literature.
2. Vietnam—Juvenile literature. [1. Cookery, Vietnamese]
I. Monroe, Judy. II. Wolfe, Robert L., ill. II. Wolfe,
Diane, ill. IV. Swofford, Jeanette. V. Title.
VI. Series.
TX724.5.V5N48    1985    641.59597    84-27816
ISBN 0-8225-0914-8 (lib. bdg.)

Manufactured in the United States of America

    5  6  7  8  9  10  93  92

**Braised chicken is moist and richly flavored with fresh ginger. (Recipe on page 37.)**

# CONTENTS

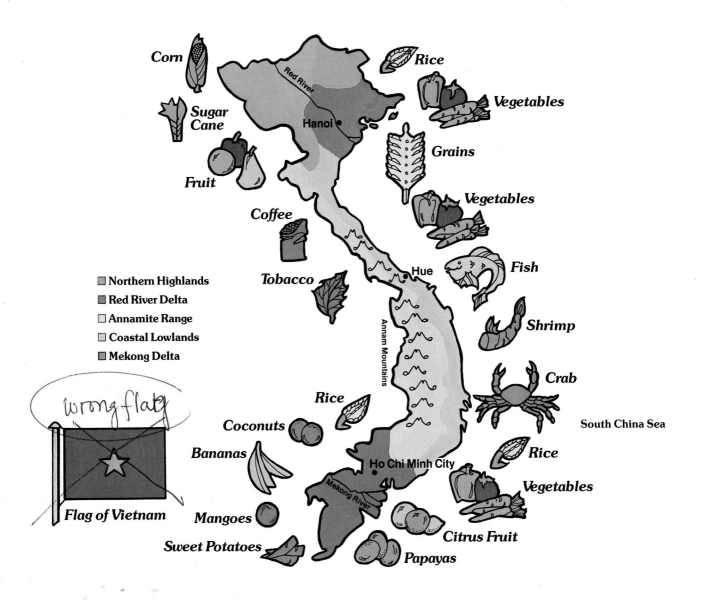

Corn

Rice

Sugar
Cane

Vegetables

Red River

Hanoi

Grains

Fruit

Vegetables

Coffee

Hue

Fish

Tobacco

■ Northern Highlands
■ Red River Delta
□ Annamite Range
□ Coastal Lowlands
■ Mekong Delta

Shrimp

Crab

Annam Mountains

South China Sea

Rice

*wrong flag*

Coconuts

Rice

Bananas

Vegetables

**Flag of Vietnam**

Ho Chi Minh City

Mekong River

Rice

Mangoes

Citrus Fruit

Sweet Potatoes

Papayas

# INTRODUCTION

Vietnam is an ancient country with deeply rooted traditions. For thousands of years, the Vietnamese people have created beautiful art objects, poetry, and architecture. The same artistic mastery is reflected in the cooking of Vietnam. Freshness and creativity are the hallmarks of this great cuisine, which uses colorful ingredients that are carefully prepared and artfully arranged.

Despite the fact that Vietnam has been ruled by other countries over the years, it has retained its own culture, including its cooking. Although there are Chinese influences, such as the use of chopsticks for eating and soy sauce for flavoring, Vietnamese cooking is definitely unlike any other. Only recently has this delightful cuisine become popular in Western countries.

## THE LAND

Vietnam is located south of China in Southeast Asia. The South China Sea surrounds Vietnam to the east and south, with the Gulf of Thailand at Vietnam's southernmost border. To Vietnam's west are the countries of Laos and Kampuchea (also known as Cambodia).

Vietnam is divided into three main land regions: the North, the South, and the Center. The three large regions can be further divided into five smaller ones. The *Northern Highlands* in northwest Vietnam are covered with jungles and forests. Because the region is so mountainous, it is sparsely populated. *The Red River Delta* extends south of the Northern Highlands to the Gulf of Tonkin. The Red River flows across this region into the Gulf. This section of Vietnam is highly populated and is also the chief agricultural area in the North. The *Annamite Range* of mountains is covered with forest and is not highly populated. From these mountains to the South China Sea are the *Coastal Lowlands.* This area produces a great deal of rice, and fishing is a major industry near the coast. The Mekong River formed the *Mekong Delta* region. This highly populated region is Vietnam's chief agricultural area.

Most Vietnamese live in the North and South regions and along the coast. In the North, people live in small villages near the rice fields. The North's two major cities are Hanoi and Haiphong. In the South, most people live in the Mekong Delta region and in Ho Chi Minh City (formerly Saigon). The Center, on the whole, is sparsely populated, but most of its inhabitants live in the city of Hue.

## HISTORY

Throughout much of its 2,000-year history, Vietnam has been subjected to rule by other, more powerful nations. The Chinese conquered Vietnam in the third century B.C. and ruled for 1,000 years. Then, after Vietnam enjoyed 900 years of independence, the French took over in 1884. Japan ruled Vietnam during World War II, but the French regained control until their defeat in 1954. That year, Vietnam was divided into two separate nations, North Vietnam and South Vietnam.

During the 1960s and 1970s, Vietnam experienced an especially difficult period of war, political unrest, and division. South Vietnam fell under Communist rule in 1975, and the Communists unified North and South Vietnam. At this time, thousands of Vietnamese fled their country, and many came to the United States. These refugees brought with them their heritage and have shared their native cuisine with Westerners. The growing population of Vietnamese people in other countries is a major reason for the growing popularity of their food.

## THE FOOD

Because of its warm climate, Vietnam produces an abundance of vegetables and fruits. These fresh ingredients are the mainstays of Vietnamese cuisine. Unlike other Asian cuisines, the Vietnamese serve many uncooked vegetables, often in the form of salads and pickles. Many fresh herbs and spices, including basil, mint, coriander, ginger, chili peppers, and garlic, give Vietnamese food its distinctive flavor and add color to many dishes. Lemon grass, a tropical grass that looks something like scallions, gives food a lemony tang.

Fish and seafood are popular, especially in the Center and South. Some of Vietnam's fish is used to make *Nuoc mem,* or fish sauce. The use of fish sauce is really the trademark of Vietnamese cooking, and it is the essential ingredient in *Nuoc cham,* a dressing and table sauce that the Vietnamese eat with all foods. Fish sauce is made by combining fish and salt in large barrels and letting it ferment for several months. The golden-brown liquid is used as a flavoring ingredient much like the Chinese use soy sauce or Westerners use salt. Despite its name and rather strong odor, fish sauce has a subtle taste that combines beautifully with other ingredients.

The Vietnamese include meat in many of their recipes. Pork is the most popular meat, and chicken, duck, and beef are eaten as well. As a high-protein substitute for meat, tofu, or soybean curd, is often used.

Vietnamese cuisine includes several different cooking methods including braising, simmering, steaming, grilling, and stir-frying. Each of these methods preserves and enhances the freshness and flavor of the food. Braising is especially popular, as it requires little heat but produces well-flavored foods in wonderful rich sauces. Little or no oil is used in Vietnamese cooking, even for stir-fried dishes.

The cuisine of Vietnam varies somewhat from region to region. In the North, less fresh produce and herbs are available due to the cooler climate. In this area, black pepper is the main seasoning. Stir-fried dishes are very popular, due probably to the influence of China, which borders directly to the north. Very hot and spicy food is found in the Center. Southern Vietnam's cooking includes a wide variety of vegetables, fruits, and spices, and sugar is a common ingredient in many dishes. The influence of India is apparent in the South, as curry dishes are very popular in that region. French influence can be found throughout Vietnam, but especially in the South, where white potatoes, asparagus, and even French bread are often-used reminders of France's long presence in Vietnam.

Despite influences from other countries, Vietnamese food is unique. We hope that you will enjoy making some of the delicious recipes in this book. You will be carrying on cooking traditions that are thousands of years old!

**Vietnamese women at an open market stall display their wares, including fresh vegetables, lemon grass, and tropical fruits.**

# HOLIDAY FEASTS IN VIETNAM

Holidays and festivals at our home in Vietnam almost always included the preparation of special foods reflecting the nature of the celebration and the time of year. *Tet-Nguyen-Den,* for instance, is a three-day festival commemorating the new year and the birth of spring.

Holiday foods are eaten throughout the three-day celebration. Each family has its own version of *Banh-chung,* a special square cake made of rice, mung beans, pork, and scallions. *Banh-chung* takes eight hours to cook and is wrapped in banana leaves and tied together with bamboo. As the cakes boiled, Mother would prepare a festive dinner made with fresh ingredients of the season including asparagus soup, stir-fried dishes of crispy new vegetables, and roast suckling pig.

The mid-autumn festival, *Tet Trung-Thu,* was special, too. It came in the eighth month when the moon was brightest, so we ate three kinds of "moon cakes." These were sweet cakes made with ingredients like mung beans, sausage, candied lotus seeds, and sesame seeds. Dishes made with snails were traditional during this festival. We would hurry through dinner to join the procession of dancing and singing people outside.

May or June was time for the rice harvest, or *Tat Lua.* This was another exciting festival when my mother would be busy making fabulous foods for my family and the many harvesters we employed.

We Vietnamese do not celebrate birthdays but rather honor our dead ancestors on the anniversary of their deaths, called *Ngay Gio.* For these occasions, food preparations would go on for two days prior to the celebration. I remember the tables seemed to groan under the weight of the many delicious foods: roast pig, four kinds of soup, four noodle dishes, many side dishes, and several desserts.

Whether a holiday feast or simply an everyday family meal, cooking and eating in Vietnam is always special, as great care is taken to prepare dishes that are attractive, nourishing, and, most of all, delicious.

# BEFORE YOU BEGIN

Cooking any dish, plain or fancy, is easier and more fun if you are familiar with its ingredients. Vietnamese cooking makes use of some ingredients that you may not know. You should also be familiar with the special terms that will be used in various recipes in this book. Therefore, *before* you start cooking any of the dishes in this book, study the following "dictionary" of special ingredients and terms very carefully. Then read through the recipe you want to try from beginning to end.

Now you are ready to shop for ingredients and to organize the cookware you will need. Once you have assembled everything, you can begin to cook. It is also very important to read *The Careful Cook* on page 44 before you start. Following these rules will make your cooking experience safe, fun, and easy.

## COOKING UTENSILS

*colander*— A bowl-shaped dish with holes in it that is used for washing or draining food

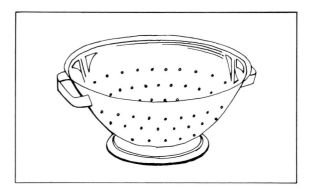

*dutch oven*— A heavy pot with a tight-fitting domed cover that is often used for cooking soups and stews

*skewer*— A thin wood or bamboo stick used to hold small pieces of meat or vegetables for broiling or grilling

*steamer*— A cooking utensil designed for cooking food with steam. Vietnamese steamers have grates or racks for holding the food and tight-fitting lids.

*tongs*— A utensil used to grasp food

*wok*— A pot with a rounded bottom and sloping sides, ideally suited for stir-fried dishes. A large skillet is a fine substitute.

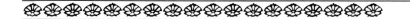
## COOKING TERMS

*boil*—To heat a liquid over high heat until bubbles form and rise rapidly to the surface

*braise*—To cook slowly in a covered pot containing liquid

*broil*—To cook directly under a heat source so that the side of the food facing the heat cooks rapidly

*brown*—To cook food quickly in fat over high heat so that the surface turns an even brown

*garnish*—To decorate with a small piece of food

*grate*—To cut into tiny pieces by rubbing the food against a grater

*grill*—To cook over hot charcoal

*marinate*—To soak food in a liquid in order to add flavor and to tenderize it

*preheat*—To allow an oven to warm up to a certain temperature before putting food in it

*seed*—To remove seeds from a food

*shred*—To tear or cut into small pieces, either by hand or with a grater

*simmer*—To cook over low heat in liquid kept just below its boiling point

*stir-fry*—To quickly cook bite-sized pieces of food in a small amount of oil over high heat

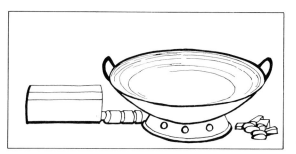

## SPECIAL INGREDIENTS

*black mushrooms*—Dried fragrant mushrooms available at Oriental groceries. They must be soaked in lukewarm water before using.

*cayenne pepper*—Ground hot red pepper

*cellophane noodles*—Thin noodles made from mung beans

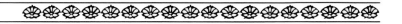

*coconut milk*—The white, milky liquid extracted from coconut meat, used to give a coconut flavor to foods. Canned coconut milk is available at Oriental groceries.

*coriander*—An herb used as a flavoring and as a decorative garnish

*crushed red pepper flakes*—Dried pieces of hot red peppers used to give a spicy flavor to foods

*curry powder*—A mixture of six or more spices that gives food a hot taste

*extra-long-grain rice*—A type of rice with very large grains. It absorbs more water than other types of rice and is dry and fluffy when cooked.

*fish sauce*—A bottled sauce made from processed fish, water, and salt. It is used widely in Vietnamese cooking and is an ingredient in the popular sauce *Nuoc cham.* Fish sauce is available at Oriental groceries and some supermarkets.

*ginger root*—A knobby, light-brown root used to flavor food

*glutinous rice*—A short-grain rice that is rather sticky when cooked; also called *sweet rice* and *sticky rice*

*jalapeño peppers*—Small, hot green chilies used to give food a spicy flavor

*lemon grass*—A tropical grass used as a flavoring in Vietnamese food. The lower, white part of the stalk is eaten. Both fresh and dried lemon grass are available in Oriental groceries. Dried lemon grass must be soaked in hot water for 1 hour, drained, and chopped.

*lumpia*—Thin skins made of flour and water used as wrappers for spring rolls

*mint*—Fresh or dried leaves of various mint plants used in cooking

*rice noodles*—Long, very thin noodles made from rice

*scallion*—A variety of green onion

*sesame seeds*—Seeds from an herb grown in tropical countries. They are often toasted before they are eaten.

*soy sauce*—A sauce made from soybeans and other ingredients that is used to flavor Oriental cooking

*tofu*—A processed curd made from soybeans

# EATING WITH CHOPSTICKS

To Westerners, chopsticks are usually the most exotic item on the list of serving utensils. But chopsticks are not difficult to manage once you have learned the basic technique. The key to using them is to hold the inside stick still while moving the outside stick back and forth. The pair then acts as pincers to pick up pieces of food.

Hold the thicker end of the first chopstick in the crook of your thumb, resting the lower part lightly against the inside of your ring finger.

Then put the second chopstick between the tips of your index and middle fingers and hold it with your thumb, much as you would hold a pencil.

Now you can make the outer chopstick move by bending your index and middle fingers toward the inside chopstick. The tips of the two sticks should come together like pincers when you bend your fingers. Once you get a feel for the technique, just keep practicing. Soon you'll be an expert!

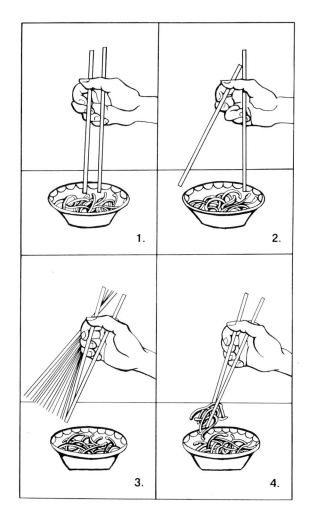

# TYPICAL VIETNAMESE MEALS

The Vietnamese serve three meals daily, plus snacks of fruit and clear soups. Breakfast, lunch, and dinner dishes are often interchangeable, although breakfast tends to be a lighter meal. A typical breakfast may consist of sticky rice with corn and coconut, sweet potatoes and peanuts, and soup. Lunch may be soup, Vietnamese meatballs, and shredded chicken-cabbage salad. Stir-fried beef with green beans, shrimp salad, sweet and sour soup, and braised chicken would make a delicious dinner. Rice is served at every meal, and *Nuoc cham* is always on every table.

Plan your Vietnamese menu by choosing dishes from the groups below. You may want to try the meals suggested above or try your own combinations. When planning your meal, remember that harmony and balance are key concepts, though contrasts are important, too. For instance, hot and cold dishes are served together, a spicy dish is eaten with bland rice, and a light soup might be teamed with an elaborate steamed dish. Use your imagination and experiment. You'll soon discover your favorites!

| *ENGLISH* | *VIETNAMESE* | *PRONUNCIATION GUIDE* |
|---|---|---|
| **Staples** | **Mon can-ban** | mawn cahn-bahn |
| Rice | Com | cohm |
| Noodles | Mien | mee-yen |
| Nuoc cham | Nuoc cham | nyuk chahm |
| | | |
| **Salads** | **Goi** | goy |
| Shredded Chicken-Cabbage Salad | Goi go | goy gah |
| Rice Noodle Salad | Bun bo sao | boon baw saw |
| Shrimp Salad | Goi tom | goy tome |

| ENGLISH | VIETNAMESE | PRONUNCIATION GUIDE |
|---|---|---|
| **Soups** | **Canh** | cang |
| Sweet and Sour Soup | Canh chuo | cang choo-ah |
| Asparagus Soup | Canh mang | cang mang |
| | | |
| **Stir-fried, Fried, and Grilled Dishes** | **Mon sao san, Sao va nuong** | mawn saw sir, saw vah nung |
| Stir-fried Cauliflower | Bong cai | bong ki |
| Stir-fried Beef with Green Beans | Thit bo sao dau | teet baw saw doe |
| Vietnamese Fried Rice | Com chien | cohm chin |
| Spring Rolls | Cha gio | chah zaw |
| Grilled Lemon Grass Beef | Bo nuong xa | baw nung sah |
| Vietnamese Meatballs | Thit nuong cha | teet nung chah |
| | | |
| **Braised and Simmered Dishes** | **Mon kho va dim** | mawn caw va zeem |
| Braised Chicken | Ga kho gung | gay caw gung |
| Sweet Potatoes with Peanuts | Khoai lang nau | kwi lang noe |
| Sticky Rice with Corn and Coconut | Soi dua | soy zoo-ah |
| | | |
| **Steamed Dishes** | **Mon hap** | mawn hup |
| Steamed Tofu | Dau hui hap | dow hu hup |
| Steamed Meat and Eggs | Trung hap voi thit | chunk hup boy teet |
| Steamed Fish | Ca hap | cah hup |

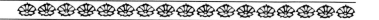

# VIETNAMESE STAPLES

## Rice/ Com

*Rice is eaten with every meal in Vietnam, where there are many different types of rice. Extra-long-grain is preferred, as it cooks up the way the Vietnamese like it — dry and fluffy.*

**2 cups extra-long-grain rice**
**2½ cups water**

1. In a deep saucepan, bring rice and water to a boil over high heat. Boil uncovered 2 to 3 minutes.
2. Cover pan and turn heat to low. Simmer rice 20 to 25 minutes or until all water is absorbed.
3. Remove from heat. Cover and let rice steam 10 minutes.
4. Fluff rice with a fork and serve hot.

*Serves 4*

## Rice Noodles/ Mein

*Rice noodles, also called rice sticks, may be added to soups or to stir-fried, steamed, or simmered dishes. They are sometimes served cold with hot vegetables and meat on top of them. Also try cellophane noodles, which are made from mung beans.*

**3 cups water**
**1 7-ounce package rice noodles**

1. In a large saucepan, bring water to a boil over high heat. Add rice noodles and return water to a boil.
2. Reduce heat to medium-high and cook noodles uncovered for 4 to 5 minutes or until soft.
3. Drain noodles in a colander and rinse in cold water. Serve immediately.

*Serves 4*

# Nuoc cham

*The Vietnamese use* Nuoc cham *the way we use salt. It is included on every table for every meal, either as a dip or a sauce to pour over a dish, and it is usually served in individual bowls. Drained carrot salad is often added to* Nuoc cham.

**2 cloves garlic, crushed**
**1 teaspoon crushed red pepper flakes**
**3 tablespoons sugar**
**2 tablespoons fresh lime juice or 4**
   **tablespoons white vinegar**
**4 tablespoons fish sauce**
**1 cup water**

1. Combine all ingredients in a small mixing bowl. Stir to dissolve sugar. (If sauce is too salty or too strong, add another tablespoon of water and stir.)
2. *Nuoc cham* will keep for up to 2 weeks refrigerated in a tightly covered glass container.

*Makes 1¹/₂ cups*

# Carrot Salad/ Goi co rot

*Carrot salad can be eaten plain with any meal, or it can be added to* Nuoc cham. *It will keep in the refrigerator for 2 to 3 days if stored in its liquid.*

**2 cups water**
**4 tablespoons white vinegar**
**2 tablespoons sugar**
**1 teaspoon salt**
**4 to 5 carrots**

1. In a small bowl, combine water, vinegar, sugar, and salt. Stir until sugar and salt are dissolved.
2. Peel the carrots and shred finely with a grater.
3. Pour liquid over shredded carrot. Cover and refrigerate overnight.
4. Drain salad in a colander. Serve at room temperature in individual bowls.

*Serves 4*

**Shredded chicken-cabbage salad** *(left)* **and shrimp salad** *(right)* **can be served either as side dishes or as light main courses. Both are especially delicious on hot summer days.**

# SALADS

Salads are an important part of the Vietnamese cuisine. The Vietnamese treasure fresh, crunchy vegetables like lettuce, cucumbers, and carrots, to which they often add fresh mint leaves and fresh coriander. Meat and seafood are often added as well.

# Shredded Chicken-Cabbage Salad/Goi go

*On special occasions, the Vietnamese start the meal with a salad such as this shredded chicken-cabbage salad. For a regular family-style meal, all dishes, including the salad, are served at once. This salad can also be served with* Nuoc cham (page 19) *in place of the lime juice dressing.*

**2 whole chicken breasts, skinned**
**½ small head cabbage, shredded**
    **(about 2 cups)**
    **juice of 1 lime**

**½ teaspoon salt**
**⅛ teaspoon cayenne pepper**
**¼ cup chopped roasted peanuts**
    **(optional)**
    **fresh coriander for garnish (optional)**

1. Rinse chicken breasts under cool running water and pat dry with paper towels.
2. Place chicken in a large saucepan with enough water to cover. Bring to a boil. Turn heat to low, cover pan, and simmer for 30 minutes.
3. Remove chicken from pan with tongs. Place on a plate and cool for 15 minutes. When chicken is cool, remove meat from bones and shred into small pieces.
4. Place shredded chicken in a large bowl and add shredded cabbage.
5. In another small bowl, mix lime juice, salt, and cayenne pepper.
6. Pour lime juice mixture over chicken and cabbage. Mix thoroughly.
7. Place salad on a serving plate and garnish with peanuts and coriander. Serve at room temperature.

*Serves 4*

# Rice Noodle Salad
## Bun bo sao

*This salad is a meal in itself. The combination of hot and cold ingredients plus the contrast between crunchy vegetables and soft noodles and meat makes this a favorite dish throughout Vietnam, where it is eaten primarily in the summer.*

1 **7-ounce package rice noodles**
½ **medium head lettuce, shredded (about 2 cups)**
½ **cucumber, peeled and thinly sliced**
2 **carrots, peeled and shredded**
2 **tablespoons vegetable oil**
½ **onion, peeled and thinly sliced**
1 **pound pork loin or beef sirloin tip, thinly sliced**
1 **stem lemon grass, finely chopped, or 1 tablespoon dried lemon grass, soaked**
1 **clove garlic, finely chopped**
½ **teaspoon sugar**
¼ **teaspoon pepper**
2 **tablespoons fish sauce**
½ **cup chopped roasted peanuts**

1. Cook and drain noodles according to directions on page 18. With a sharp knife or scissors, cut noodles into shorter lengths.
2. Divide rice noodles between 4 small bowls. Divide lettuce, cucumber, and carrot and add to each bowl. Set aside.
3. In a large skillet, heat oil over high heat for 1 minute. Add onion and cook, stirring frequently, for 2 to 3 minutes or until tender.
4. Add meat and stir. Add lemon grass, garlic, sugar, and pepper. Cook, stirring frequently, 3 to 5 minutes or until meat is thoroughly cooked. Add fish sauce and stir well.
5. Divide cooked meat mixture between the 4 bowls and sprinkle 2 tablespoons peanuts over each.
6. Serve with *Nuoc cham* (page 19).

*Serves 4*

# Shrimp Salad/
## Goi tom

*Although most salads originated in South Vietnam, this salad is from the north. It is traditionally served on special occasions. Shrimp salad is a pretty dish with a sweet/sour/hot flavor the Vietnamese love.*

**1 cucumber, peeled and chopped**
**3 carrots, peeled and grated**
**2 teaspoons sugar**
**3 cups water**
**1 pound fresh shrimp, peeled and deveined, or 1 pound frozen shrimp, thawed**
**2 tablespoons fish sauce**
**2 teaspoons lime juice or white vinegar**
**1 jalapeño pepper, seeded and chopped, or ½ teaspoon crushed red pepper flakes**
**1 tablespoon sesame seeds**
**fresh coriander for garnish (optional)**

1. In a large mixing bowl, combine cucumber, carrots, and 1 teaspoon sugar. Cover and let stand at room temperature for 15 minutes.
2. In a large saucepan, bring 3 cups water to a boil over high heat. Add shrimp and boil 4 to 5 minutes or until tender, bright pink, and curled tightly. Drain well in a colander and set aside in a covered dish.
3. Place cucumber-carrot mixture in a colander and drain well. Return to mixing bowl. Add shrimp to cucumber-carrot mixture and stir.
4. In a small bowl, mix together 1 teaspoon sugar, fish sauce, lime juice, and pepper. Stir well. Pour mixture over shrimp and vegetables.
5. Place sesame seeds in a small skillet. (Do not add oil.) Turn heat to medium and cook seeds about 1 to 3 minutes or until they begin to turn light gold. Stir frequently, being careful not to burn. When seeds are golden, set pan aside.
6. Place salad on a serving plate and sprinkle with toasted sesame seeds. Garnish with fresh coriander and serve cold or at room temperature.

*Serves 4*

The Vietnamese like to fill their soups with colorful ingredients. Delicate, creamy asparagus soup *(left)* and zesty sweet and sour soup *(right)* are two Vietnamese favorites.

# SOUPS

In Vietnam, soups are usually served over rice and garnished with coriander. There is a wide variety of soups in Vietnam, some thin and delicate, others hearty and thick with meats and noodles. Either way, a soup is included with almost every Vietnamese meal.

## Sweet and Sour Soup/ Canh chuo

*This soup combines the sweetness of pineapple with the sour taste of vinegar. The pineapple, native to Vietnam, is considered a vegetable in that country. For this soup, use fresh or frozen sole, cod, or haddock fillets. (If frozen, thaw before using.)*

**1  pound fish fillets, cut into bite-sized pieces**
**¼ teaspoon pepper**
**2  tablespoons oil**
**3  tomatoes, cut into 8 wedges each**
**1  teaspoon sugar**
**2  10¾-ounce cans (about 3 cups) chicken broth**
**1  20-ounce can chunk pineapple, drained thoroughly**
**2  tablespoons white vinegar**
**2  tablespoons chopped fresh mint leaves or 1 teaspoon dried mint**
**¼ cup chopped scallions**

1. In a large mixing bowl, mix together fish and pepper. Cover and let stand at room temperature for 30 minutes.
2. In a large saucepan, heat oil over medium heat for 2 minutes. Add tomatoes and sugar. Cook 2 minutes or until tomatoes are soft.
3. Add chicken broth, pineapple, and fish. Bring to a boil over high heat. Reduce heat to medium and simmer 5 minutes or until fish is cooked through and tender.
4. Add vinegar, mint, and scallions.
5. Serve over hot rice or in individual soup bowls with rice on the side.

*Serves 4*

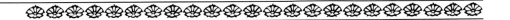

# Asparagus Soup/
## Canh mang

*Asparagus was brought to Vietnam by the French and quickly became a very popular vegetable. The Vietnamese call asparagus "Western bamboo" because it looks something like bamboo shoots. This soup is also delicious when made with broccoli, cauliflower, brussels sprouts, or peas.*

**1 egg**
**2 tablespoons cornstarch**
**¼ cup water**
**2 10¾-ounce cans (about 3 cups) chicken broth**
**½ pound fresh asparagus, cut into bite-sized pieces or 1 10-ounce package frozen chopped asparagus, thawed**
**1 whole chicken breast, skinned, boned, and cut into bite-sized pieces**
**2 teaspoons fish sauce**

1. Beat egg in a small bowl. Set aside.
2. In another small bowl, mix cornstarch and water to make a paste. Set aside.
3. In a large saucepan, bring broth to a boil over high heat. Add asparagus and reduce heat to medium. Cover and cook for 3 minutes or until crisp-tender.
4. Add chicken. Cook for 3 to 4 minutes or until chicken and asparagus are thoroughly cooked.
5. Add fish sauce and cornstarch paste. (If cornstarch has started to separate from the water, stir well before adding.) Stir well about 1 to 2 minutes or until soup starts to thicken.
6. Add beaten egg a little at a time, stirring constantly. Cook for 30 seconds.
7. Serve hot over rice, or in individual soup bowls with rice on the side.

*Serves 4*

# STIR-FRIED, FRIED, AND GRILLED DISHES

The Vietnamese enjoy stir-fried dishes because this quick-cooking method produces crunchy vegetables and fresh-tasting meat. Before stir-frying, be sure you have all your ingredients ready and within reach. In Vietnam, woks are generally used for stir-frying and frying, although French influence has made the use of ordinary skillets fairly common, too.

Grilling is another important Vietnamese cooking method. In Vietnam, food is grilled over a fire on the kitchen floor and then brought to the table. You can use your broiler for the grilled dishes in this book.

# Stir-fried Cauliflower/ Bong cai

*Cauliflower was introduced by the French in the 19th century. Because it looks like a big flower and is from the cabbage family, the Vietnamese call cauliflower "the flower of the cabbage." You may substitute any chopped vegetable for the cauliflower.*

**1  medium head cauliflower**
**1  tablespoon vegetable oil**
**1  small onion, sliced**
**½  teaspoon pepper**
**1  tablespoon fish sauce**
**¼  cup chopped scallions**

1. Break cauliflower into bite-sized florets.
2. In a large skillet or wok, heat oil over high heat for 1 minute.
3. Add onion and continue frying over high heat, stirring constantly, for 3 minutes or until onion is tender.
4. Add cauliflower. Cook 2 to 3 minutes, stirring constantly. Add pepper and fish sauce and mix well. Cover and cook another 2 minutes or until cauliflower is crisp-tender.
5. Add scallions and stir. Serve hot with rice.

*Serves 4*

**Stir-fried cauliflower** *(bottom)* **and stir-fried beef with green beans** *(top)* **are delicious when served with hot rice.**

# Stir-fried Beef with Green Beans/ Thit bo sao dau

*Beef was not a regular part of the Vietnamese diet until it became more widely accepted during French rule. This typical family dish can be made with chopped celery, broccoli, or cauliflower in place of the green beans.*

**1 clove garlic, finely chopped**
**¼ teaspoon pepper**
**1 teaspoon cornstarch or flour**
**1 teaspoon vegetable oil**
**1 pound sirloin tip, thinly sliced**
**3 tablespoons vegetable oil**
**½ medium onion, sliced**
**2 cups green beans, ends removed**
**and cut into bite-sized pieces**
**¼ cup water or chicken broth**
**1 teaspoon soy sauce**

1. In a large mixing bowl, combine garlic, pepper, cornstarch, and 1 teaspoon oil. Add beef and mix well. Cover and let stand at room temperature for 30 minutes.
2. In a wok or large skillet, heat 2 tablespoons oil over high heat for 1 minute. Add meat. Stir quickly over high heat for about 2 minutes or until beef begins to turn brown. Remove from pan and place in a large bowl. Set aside.
3. Wash wok or skillet and dry thoroughly.
4. Heat 1 tablespoon oil over high heat for 1 minute. Add onion and cook, stirring frequently, for 2 minutes or until nearly tender.
5. Add green beans and stir well. Add water or broth, cover, and turn heat to low. Simmer for 4 to 5 minutes or until beans are crisp-tender.
6. Uncover and add soy sauce and beef. Cook over medium heat for 1 to 2 minutes, stirring constantly, until heated through.
7. Serve over hot rice.

*Serves 4*

# Vietnamese Fried Rice/ Com chien

*Fried rice originated in China. This version, flavored with fish sauce, is uniquely Vietnamese. It is a great way to use up leftovers, as just about any kind of meat or vegetable can be added to or substituted for the ham and peas.*

**2 eggs**
**4 tablespoons vegetable oil**
**½ medium onion, chopped**
**1 carrot, chopped**
**½ cup fresh green peas or frozen peas, thawed**
**1 cup diced cooked ham**
**½ teaspoon pepper**
**1 teaspoon sugar**
**2 teaspoons fish sauce**
**1 teaspoon soy sauce**
**4 cups cold cooked rice**

1. In a small bowl, beat eggs well.
2. In a large skillet, heat 1 tablespoon oil over medium heat for 1 minute. Add beaten eggs and cook quickly, scrambling them with a spoon. Place eggs on a plate and set aside.
3. Clean skillet. Heat 3 tablespoons oil over medium heat for 1 minute. Add onions and cook uncovered for 2 minutes, stirring occasionally. Add carrots and peas, stir well, and cook 5 minutes, covered.
4. Add ham, pepper, sugar, fish sauce, and soy sauce and stir well.
5. Add rice, breaking apart any clumps. Mix well and cook uncovered 7 to 8 minutes or until heated through.
6. Just before serving, add scrambled eggs and mix well. Serve hot.

*Serves 4*

Elegant spring rolls *(left)* and colorful Vietnamese fried rice *(right)* are festive party foods.

# Spring Rolls/
## Cha gio

*Vietnamese spring rolls are similar to
Chinese egg rolls but are usually rolled
in much thinner wrappers called rice
papers. Rice papers are transparent,
paper-thin, and very difficult to work with,
and they are not readily available. For these
reasons, we suggest instead using lumpia,
a thin flour-and-water wrapper that's a fine
substitute for rice papers. Look for lumpia
in Oriental groceries, or ask your super-
market to special-order some.*

3½ ounces (one-half package)
       cellophane or rice noodles
1 egg
1 pound ground pork
3 carrots, peeled and shredded
1 small onion, chopped
1½ teaspoons fish sauce
½ teaspoon pepper
¼ cup chopped scallions
1 1-pound package lumpia, thawed
    (about 25 wrappers)

½ cup vegetable oil

1. Soak noodles in hot water according to
package directions. When soft, drain and
cut into 2-inch lengths with a sharp
knife or scissors.
2. In a large bowl, beat egg well. Add
noodles, pork, carrots, onion, fish sauce,
pepper, and scallions. Mix well.
3. Place 1 wrapper on a flat surface. Cover
remaining wrappers with a slightly damp
kitchen towel so they don't dry out. Roll
up according to directions on page 33.
4. In a large skillet or wok, heat oil over
medium heat for 1 minute. Carefully
place 3 rolls into oil and fry slowly about
10 minutes or until golden brown. Turn
and fry other side 10 minutes.
5. Keep fried rolls warm in a 200° oven
as you fry remaining rolls.
6. Serve hot with individual bowls of
*Nuoc cham* for dipping. Cut each spring
roll into 4 pieces or wrap spring roll plus
a few sprigs of fresh mint and coriander
in a lettuce leaf, dip, and eat.

*Makes 25 spring rolls*

# HOW TO WRAP SPRING ROLLS

1. Have ready 1 beaten egg and a pastry brush.
2. Place about 1½ tablespoons of filling mixture just below center of skin.
3. Fold bottom edge over filling.
4. Fold in the two opposite edges so that they overlap.
5. Brush top edge corner with beaten egg. Roll up toward top edge and press edge to seal. Repeat with remaining wrappers.

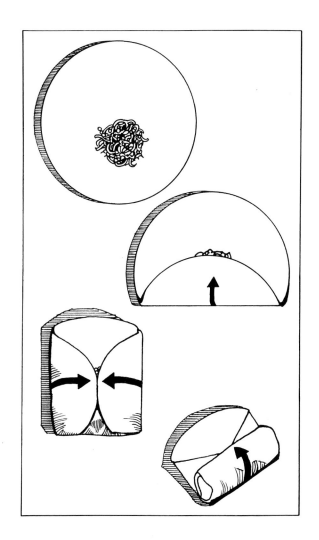

**Grilled lemon grass beef** *(left)* can be served wrapped in lettuce with scallions, mint, and coriander. **Vietnamese meatballs** *(right)* make tasty appetizers.

# Grilled Lemon Grass Beef/
## Bo nuong xa

*Grilled lemon grass beef is usually served at summer picnics and is always found at parties and celebrations. This is a southern speciality; the North Vietnamese usually grill pork instead of beef. The drawing below shows how to thread the meat onto the skewers.*

1½ **pounds sirloin tip, thinly sliced**
  2 **teaspoons sugar**
  2 **tablespoons soy sauce**
  1 **teaspoon pepper**
  2 **cloves garlic, finely chopped**
  2 **teaspoons sesame seeds**
  2 **stems lemon grass, finely chopped, or 2 tablespoons dried lemon grass, soaked**
12 **romaine lettuce leaves (optional)**
  2 **teaspoons each chopped fresh mint, coriander, and scallions (optional)**

1. Mix first 7 ingredients in a large mixing bowl. Cover and refrigerate 4 hours or overnight.
2. Soak 12 small wooden skewers in water until ready to use.
3. Preheat oven to broil or have an adult start the charcoal grill.
4. Thread beef slices onto skewers accordian-style. When oven is preheated or charcoal ready, broil or grill beef for 6 to 8 minutes or until done, turning often so that all sides are cooked evenly.
5. Serve hot from skewers or remove meat from a skewer and place on a lettuce leaf. Add ½ teaspoon each of chopped fresh mint, coriander, and scallions. Roll up leaf, dip in *Nuoc cham,* and serve.

*Serves 4*

# Vietnamese Meatballs/ Thit nuong cha

*Meatballs are very popular in Vietnam and are made with pork, beef, chicken, and even shrimp. In Vietnam, they're eaten for breakfast, lunch, or dinner, and they are usually grilled over charcoal. For parties, serve meatballs as appetizers—put a toothpick through each, dip in Nuoc cham, and enjoy.*

**1   pound ground pork**
**½  small onion, finely chopped**
**½  cup chopped scallions**
**½  teaspoon fish sauce**
**½  teaspoon soy sauce**
**¼  teaspoon pepper**
**½  teaspoon sugar**
**    fresh coriander for garnish (optional)**

1. Preheat oven to 300°.
2. Combine all ingredients in a large mixing bowl. Mix well.
3. With your hands, roll the meat mixture into 1-inch balls. (It's easier to do this if your hands are wet.) Place meatballs in a 9- by 9-inch baking dish and bake uncovered 30 minutes.
4. Garnish with fresh coriander and serve hot or at room temperature.

*Makes about 25 meatballs*

# BRAISED AND SIMMERED DISHES

Braising is the most popular cooking method for meat in Vietnam. This slow-cooking method produces tender, flavorful meat in savory sauces. It is an especially good method for cooking tougher cuts of meat.

Simmered dishes are cooked rather slowly at a temperature just below boiling. Flavors have a chance to mingle, and dishes are always moist. In Vietnam, braising and simmering are usually done over charcoal, but the top of your stove will work just as well.

# Braised Chicken/
## Ga kho gung

*If you are served chicken in Vietnam, you know you are well liked, as chicken there is rather expensive. This particular chicken dish is also served to new mothers as a special treat and to help restore their strength. Dark-meat chicken is very good for braising, but white meat is fine, too.*

**1 tablespoon finely chopped fresh ginger**
**¼ teaspoon salt**
**¼ teaspoon pepper**
**8 chicken thighs or legs, skinned**
**2 tablespoons vegetable oil**
**½ small onion, chopped**
**2 cups water**
**1 teaspoon sugar**
**2 tablespoons fish sauce**

1. In a small bowl, mix ginger, salt, and pepper. Rub mixture into chicken pieces and cover. Let stand at room temperature for ½ hour.

2. In a large skillet, heat oil over high heat for 1 minute. Add onion and cook uncovered for 2 to 3 minutes or until tender. Stir frequently.
3. Add chicken, water, sugar, and fish sauce. Cover and reduce heat to low. Simmer for 45 minutes or until chicken is tender.
4. Serve hot with rice or noodles.

*Serves 4*

**Chopped peanuts add crunch to two nutritious breakfast dishes—sweet potatoes with peanuts** *(left)* **and sticky rice with corn and coconut** *(right).*

# Sticky Rice with Corn and Coconut/ Soi dua

*Sticky rice, also known as glutinous or sweet rice, is a kind of short-grain rice. When cooked, it is quite sticky and can be molded into shapes. Although it is not really sweet tasting, the Vietnamese often use it in desserts. Here it is used in this hearty breakfast dish. You may substitute any chopped vegetable for the corn and regular short-grain rice can substitute for the glutinous rice.*

**3 cups water**
**2 cups glutinous rice**
**1 8-ounce can corn, drained well**
**1 cup canned coconut milk or
    whole milk**
**2 teaspoons salt**
**4 teaspoons sugar**
**¼ cup sesame seeds**
**½ cup chopped roasted peanuts**

1. In a large saucepan, bring water and rice to a boil over high heat. Turn heat to low and cover. Simmer for 20 to 25 minutes or until water is absorbed and rice is tender.
2. Add corn, coconut milk, 1 teaspoon salt, and 2 teaspoons sugar and mix well. Cover and keep warm over very low heat.
3. Place sesame seeds in a small skillet. (Do not add oil.) Turn heat to medium and cook seeds about 2 to 3 minutes or until they begin to turn light gold. Stir frequently, being careful not to let seeds burn. When seeds are golden, pour into a small mixing bowl.
4. To sesame seeds, add 1 teaspoon salt, 2 teaspoons sugar, and peanuts and mix well.
5. To serve, spoon rice mixture into individual bowls. Sprinkle 2 to 3 teaspoons of peanut-sesame seed mixture over top of each. Serve hot, cold, or at room temperature.

*Serves 4*

## Sweet Potatoes with Peanuts/Khoai lang nau

*The sweet potato is native to Vietnam and is a very popular food—as basic to the Vietnamese diet as rice. This is a common breakfast dish in the southern part of Vietnam.*

**2 cups water**
**½ cup sugar**
**2 medium sweet potatoes, peeled and cut into chunks**
**½ teaspoon salt**
**¼ teaspoon pepper**
**¼ cup chopped roasted peanuts**

1. In a large saucepan, bring water and sugar to a boil over high heat.
2. Add sweet potatoes and cover. Turn heat to low and simmer for 10 minutes or until tender.
3. In a colander, drain sweet potatoes and place in a serving bowl.
4. Add salt and pepper and stir. Sprinkle with peanuts and serve hot.

*Serves 4*

# STEAMED DISHES

The Vietnamese menu includes many dishes that are steamed, or cooked over boiling water. This method keeps food fresh tasting and attractive looking and also helps food retain most of its nutrients. If you don't have an Oriental metal steamer, set a heat-resistant bowl containing the food to be steamed into a flat pan. Pour about ½ cup of boiling water into the pan. Cover the bowl, and place the pan and the dish in a preheated 350° oven for the amount of time specified in the recipe.

## Steamed Tofu/ Dau hui hap

*Tofu is a good non-meat protein source for vegetarians. This is a family dish, eaten at least once a week. Vietnam's many Buddhists eat this tofu dish on the first, fifteenth, and last days of the lunar month, when no meat is allowed.*

**1 1-pound package firm-style tofu,
     cut into chunks**
**2 tablespoons soy sauce**
**½ cup chopped scallions**
**¼ teaspoon salt**
**¼ teaspoon pepper**
**¼ teaspoon crushed red pepper flakes
     (optional)**

1. Place all ingredients in a heat-resistant bowl and mix well.
2. Place ½ cup water in steamer and bring to a boil over high heat. Place bowl with tofu into steamer. Cover and steam over medium heat for 25 minutes.
3. Serve hot, with rice or plain.

*Serves 4*

**Steamed meat and eggs** *(left)* **and steamed tofu** *(right)* **are not only tasty but also extremely nutritious.**

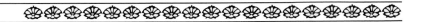

# Steamed Meat and Eggs/
## Trung hap voi thit

*Steamed meat and eggs is a great favorite with Vietnamese children. As this dish steams, a delicious sauce is produced. Be sure to spoon this sauce over rice when serving.*

  4 **black mushrooms**
  1 **cup hot water**
  1 **pound ground pork**
3½ **ounces (one-half package) rice noodles or cellophane noodles**
  4 **eggs**
½ **small onion, chopped**
½ **teaspoon salt**
½ **teaspoon fish sauce**
¼ **teaspoon pepper**

1. In a small bowl, soak black mushrooms in hot water for 20 minutes. Drain well in a colander and then squeeze with your hands to remove remaining water.
2. In a large skillet, fry pork over medium-high heat. Stir frequently to break up meat and to brown evenly, about 5 to 7 minutes or until pork is no longer pink.
3. With a sharp knife, remove tough stems from mushrooms. Chop mushroom caps into small pieces.
4. Cook and drain noodles according to directions on page 18.
5. In a large heat-resistant bowl, beat eggs well. Add mushrooms, pork, onion, salt, fish sauce, pepper, and noodles and mix.
6. Place ½ cup water in steamer and bring to a boil over high heat. Place bowl with meat-and-egg mixture in steamer. Cover and steam over medium heat for 30 minutes or until eggs are set.
7. Serve hot with rice for lunch or dinner.

*Serves 4*

# Steamed Fish/
## Ca hap

*For this recipe, you can use sole, cod, haddock, or any other white fish. If you use frozen fish, thaw thoroughly before mixing with the other ingredients.*

**2** pounds fish fillets, cut into bite-sized
    pieces
**2** teaspoons fish sauce
**⅛** teaspoon pepper
**1** clove garlic, chopped
**1** teaspoon finely chopped fresh
    ginger
**½** cup sliced fresh mushrooms
**3** stalks celery, cut into chunks
**1** tomato, cut into chunks
**¼** cup chopped scallions

1. Place all ingredients in a heat-resistant
bowl and mix well.
2. Place ½ cup water in steamer and bring
to a boil over high heat. Place bowl with
fish mixture into steamer. Cover and steam
over medium heat for 40 minutes.
3. Serve hot with rice. Spoon juices over
fish and rice.

*Serves 4*

**As *ca hap* steams, the fish remains delicate and
flavorful, and the vegetables stay fresh and crunchy.**

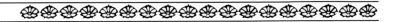

# THE CAREFUL COOK

Whenever you cook, there are certain safety rules you must always keep in mind. Even experienced cooks follow these rules when they are in the kitchen.

1. Always wash your hands before handling food.
2. Thoroughly wash all raw vegetables and fruits to remove dirt, chemicals, and insecticides.
3. Use a cutting board when cutting up vegetables and fruits. Don't cut them up in your hand! And be sure to cut in a direction *away* from you and your fingers.
4. Long hair or loose clothing can easily catch fire if brought near the burners of a stove. If you have long hair, tie it back before you start cooking.
5. Turn all pot handles toward the back of the stove so that you will not catch your sleeve or jewelry on them. This is especially important when younger brothers and sisters are around. They could easily knock off a pot and get burned.

6. Always use a pot holder to steady hot pots or to take pans out of the oven. Don't use a wet cloth on a hot pan because the steam it produces could burn you.
7. Lift the lid of a steaming pot with the opening away from you so that you will not get burned.
8. If you get burned, hold the burn under cold running water. Do not put grease or butter on it. Cold water helps to take the heat out, but grease or butter will only keep it in.
9. If grease or cooking oil catches fire, throw baking soda or salt at the bottom of the flame to put it out. (Water will *not* put out a grease fire.) Call for help and try to turn all the stove burners to "off."

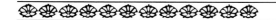 

## METRIC CONVERSION CHART

| WHEN YOU KNOW | | MULTIPLY BY | TO FIND | |
|---|---|---|---|---|
| **MASS (weight)** | | | | |
| ounces | (oz) | 28.0 | grams | (g) |
| pounds | (lb) | 0.45 | kilograms | (kg) |
| **VOLUME** | | | | |
| teaspoons | (tsp) | 5.0 | milliliters | (ml) |
| tablespoons | (Tbsp) | 15.0 | milliliters | |
| fluid ounces | (oz) | 30.0 | milliliters | |
| cup | (c) | 0.24 | liters | (l) |
| pint | (pt) | 0.47 | liters | |
| quart | (qt) | 0.95 | liters | |
| gallon | (gal) | 3.8 | liters | |
| **TEMPERATURE** | | | | |
| Fahrenheit | (°F) | 5/9 (after | Celsius | (°C) |
| temperature | | subtracting 32) | temperature | |

## COMMON MEASURES AND THEIR EQUIVALENTS

3 teaspoons = 1 tablespoon
8 tablespoons = ½ cup
2 cups = 1 pint
2 pints = 1 quart
4 quarts = 1 gallon
16 ounces = 1 pound

# INDEX

*(recipes indicated by* **bold face** *type)*

## ABOUT THE AUTHORS

**Chi Nguyen** was born near Hanoi, North Vietnam, and with her family moved to Saigon in 1954. Nguyen graduated from the University of Saigon School of Pharmacy, and she and her family left Vietnam in 1975. Now a resident of Minneapolis, Minnesota, Nguyen enjoys cooking native Vietnamese dishes for her family and her friends.

**Judy Monroe,** born in Duluth, Minnesota, learned Vietnamese cooking while in high school and has since mastered several Southeast Asian cuisines. A graduate of the University of Minnesota, Monroe is currently a biomedical librarian and a freelance writer. In her spare time, she enjoys ethnic cooking, baking, gardening, and reading.

**easy menu ethnic cookbooks**